Dynamic
DOER

Other Books by John Gillette:

Discovering God's Sufficiency
Going Beyond Ourselves and Experiencing the Supernatural
Pastoral Health Care — Part One

Discovering God's Love
Confirming God's Love through the evidence of historical facts
Pastoral Health Care — Part Two

Discovering God's Counsel
Applying his spiritual solution to meet difficult trials
Pastoral Health Care — Part Three

Discovering God's Kingdom
Finding a way to understand ourselves in a complex world
Pastoral Health Care — Part Four

Discovering God's Heart
Finding God's heart pulse is our daily challenge
Pastoral Health Care — Part Five

Glorify God
Christianity is a divine vitality
Divine Dialogue — Part One

Exceptional Explanations
Reality is not a hoax. Scriptural knowledge will provide secure answers
Divine Dialogue — Part Three

Triple Torch
Discovering God's favor in a triplet's life
Divine Dialogue — Part Four

Spiritual Solutions
Discovering God's presence and perspective in difficult times
Divine Dialogue — Part Five

"Biblical Christianity is Jesus Christ"

DIVINE DIALOGUE PART 2

Dynamic DOER

"BE YE DOERS OF THE WORD AND NOT HEARERS ONLY, DECEIVING YOUR OWN SELVES"

JAMES 1:22

JOHN F. GILLETTE
Author of Pastoral Health Care Series

Chapbook Press

Schuler Books
2660 28th Street SE
Grand Rapids MI 49512

www.schulerbooks.com/chapbook-press

Dynamic Doer

Copyright ©2020 — Dr. John F. Gillette, Ph.D., D. Min.
All rights reserved. Published 2020.
Printed at Schuler Books, Chapbook Press, Grand Rapids, Michigan, in the United States of America.

Distribution contact:at jjgillette@comcast.net.

ISBN 13: 9781948237437

Library of Congress Control Number: 2020904301

Cover photo: Pexels.com
Typist: Michael Sharp
Cover Design: Frank Gutbrod Graphic Design
Interior Design and Layout: Sophia Gutbrod

Printed in the United States of America

*This book is lovingly dedicated
to my friends of the
Pastoral Health Care Ministry.*

John Gillette's writings flow from a lifetime of experience. It is one thing to write out of a knowledge based on research. It is an entirely different thing to write out of a depth of life experience. John has both. As a pastor who has cared for the needs of a congregation, as a husband who has experienced the tragic loss of a wife, and as a child of God who has walked through the joys and pain of following the Lord, John has so much to offer in this series. From the opening pages, through to the very end, you will be blessed by the insights, loving tone and encouragement you receive from this series. God has used John greatly in ministry and will continue to use him through this life-giving series.

—*Josh Mateer, D. Min.*

True, illustrative, practical stories are like windows that unlock Bible truths and promises. Along with a masterfully orchestrated short stories should come the truth that God's Word and love has been experienced by His servants as they partner with Him in the work of rebuilding the Kingdom. A gifted teacher, Dr. Gillette lives an ordinary life abiding in Christ and being an obedient servant of the Lord. As he sees God working in his life, and in the lives of those to whom he ministers, his faith is refreshed and he is encouraged to press on through life's uncertainties.

Only a lifetime dedicated to nurturing, ministering, teaching, and keen insight through the power of the Holy Spirit, can produce such poignant stories that teach and challenge.

—*Mulonge M. Kalumbula, Ph.D.*

John's books give us hope and light. He reminds us that through Jesus we are never alone. I have certainly needed that reminder in my life and in my practice. In holding a patient's hand, and helping them through a condition or disease, reminding them that they are never alone has become the greatest gift of health care.

—*Linda M. Kunce, D.C.*

The series reminds me that Jesus knows what it's like to live in a human body. I have received Jesus and His forgiveness, but as the book suggests, I also have the power from the Holy Spirit. His books have encouraged me to gain courage through prayer and confidence in Jesus to meet my needs. John's honesty is very special to read as he reflects on his own life and struggles. I like his explanation that "the soul is where the emotions are and the mind is where the thinking takes place". It's been good for me to read that God works through weakness, and learn that John found God with him in the middle of the struggles.

—*Arvid W. Vandyke, Ed.D.*

Discovering God's Counsel is a book full of great spiritual truths from someone who has developed a very close and deep relationship with Jesus through his life. John provides a meaningful and inspirational testimony, with examples from his own experiences, of how relying on God's Word and promises can give you the power, hope, and peace you need to overcome life's struggles and challenges. The Scriptures he chose in his book were on point and helpful. It was an enjoyable and wonderful read.

—*Thoa Reyna, J.D.*

John has written a user-friendly and practical series for anyone desiring to live beyond the superficial and venture into the supernatural. The world needs this *Pastoral Health Care Series*. Pastors and followers of Jesus need the insights from John's lifetime experience of walking with God and caring for His people through the power of the Holy Spirit. John has brilliantly show that God is enough, God's love is real, God's counsel is enduring, and God reigns supremely. This important series will serve both the church and the world for many years to come.

—*Kizombo Kalumbula, Jr., Ph.D.*

John Gillette's inspirational book *Glorify God* is a fantastic reminder of how I should approach each day and how blessed I am. It is so easy to get caught up in the hustle and bustle of today's lifestyle and forget what is really important. John's encouraging words are a great reminder of how we all should live each day. I have a great foundation of faith nut John's book helps me to remember what is important and allows me to reflect on the wonderful things I have and to be gracious to God for those blessings.

— *Tammy Thelen, Au.D., CCC-A*

Note from the Author

I believe in God's sovereignty and compassion. I am learning to let go of self and to hold onto someone that can do whatever he pleases. Sometimes life is cruel, sometimes it is full of suffering, physically and psychologically. A spiritual solution to meet difficult trials has become my goal. God's Word carries with it no uncertainties. I want it to saturate my mind and heart..

The *Pastoral Health Care Series* and *Divine Dialogue Series* was created through unexpected heart disease (open heart surgery), cancer (medication and surgery), a stroke and major head injury after a car accident that also resulted in the death of my wife.

It is helping me to develop and adequate level to supernatural, psychological and physical adjustments. It may help you as well. It has brought me security.

—*John F. Gillette, D.S.M., D.Min*

Table of Contents

CHAPTER 1
Jesus' Presence | 1

CHAPTER 2
Jesus' Plan | 8

CHAPTER 3
Jesus' Promise | 14

CHAPTER 4
Jesus' Power | 21

CHAPTER 5
Jesus' Perspective | 26

CHAPTER 6
Jesus' Prayer | 40

CHAPTER 7
Jesus' Prescription | 53

CHAPTER 8
Jesus' Priority | 60

CHAPTER 9
Jesus' Path | 68

CHAPTER 10
Jesus' Prophecy | 74

ACKNOWLEDGEMENTS | 79

ABOUT THE AUTHOR | 80

CHAPTER 1

Jesus' Presence

According to the Apostle Peter (I Peter 2:25) and the Apostle Paul (Acts 13:35), Psalm 16 relates to Christ. It expresses his feeling of human emotion. During his suffering and death, he called on God to preserve him. The first verse gives a brief but deep description of the character of his entire walk on earth. "O God on thee do I put my trust" (v1). The last verse is a summary of his path of life "at thy presence is fullness of joy" (v11). From my childhood, I have followed Jesus. My desire is the same as his. "O God in thee do I put my trust" (v1). In good and bad days, I want to experience continual strength, support and steadfastness provided by him.

I discovered Psalm 16 in my teens. I was graduating from high school and was asked by my church to share a personal testimony. I prayed for a verse that would become my constant companion through life. God gave me Psalm 16:8. It has lifted me up and helped me to confront my weaknesses. When I feel a sense of inadequacy or have a problem with protectionism or sensitivity, I am learning to respond to this text. I will achieve what God wants me to. My prayer is "thy will be done." I began to think about some of my weaknesses that are a hindrance to my spiritual growth and decided to devote my time to praising God instead. My favorite verse gave me the goal and foundation to build upon. Praising him moved me from the negative to the positive. The weaknesses that became hindrances are in the process of being moved out of my picture of life.

"I have set the Lord always before me, because he is at my right hand, I shall not be moved" (Psalm 16:8). I know this refers to the testimony of Jesus Christ. My loyalty is given to him. He is my model to follow. In the first phrase, "I have set the Lord always before me" gives me continued strength. In my inadequacy, I praise God for his inheritance. I belong to him and he is my Savior and Lord. I am his heir and I have a great inheritance. I belong to his kingdom (Matthew 25:34). I have citizenship on earth and heaven. My stay down here is short and is directed through my eternal destiny. It is a decision of trust. I am able to overcome all my inadequacies because I belong to the King. He provides the way. It is possible because of his death (Hebrews 9:15). In his death, he took care of the sin problem. My sin is forgiven. "I have come short of his glory" (Romans 3:23). He provides the way (John 14:6) to be a part of his family (John 1:12). The Holy Spirit has sealed it (Ephesians 1:13-14). He placed his approval and authority on it. No one can remove the seal. Since I am in Christ, I have been transformed (I Corinthians 15:50-53). Since he has given me faith (Galatians 3:18, 22), I can and will overcome. I have been promised continual strength that flows into my bloodstream through the Holy Spirit

Praise God for his goodness extended to me. I have reached out to him. "Thou art my Lord . .

. I take delight in you" (Psalm 16:2,3). In doing this, I have learned that he has created the initial desire. In spite of my protectionism that creates a hindrance, he is present. He is always near. I have to re-learn that God causes all things to work together for good to those who love him (Romans 8:28). I live in a contaminated world and it rubs off. Sometimes my protectionism has moved to obsession. Bad things will happen and I cannot stop them. Creation was completely good when it came from God's hand. When negative circumstances occur, I have to learn to be watchful but not obsessed and do my best. I have to remember that the negative never has the last word.

    I praise God for his counsel given to me. Communion with the Holy Spirit has been instructive and encouraging. God is near when you feel him and when you don't feel him. He is there when I sense him and when I don't sense him. He counsels with his promises that he is going to accomplish something if I think so or not. My negatives are part of his positive program. God knows where he wants to take me and how he wants to get me there. As I become intimately involved with him, my protectionism will be placed into his hands. I am assured that he is present with the people I am concerned with and to me.

The last part of the verse says "I shall not be moved" (Psalm 16:8). This has brought the promise of continued steadfastness. I praise God for his preservation. He has the power to give life and to maintain it. It is his power working in me that makes my heart beat. In spite of my sensitivity that sometimes creates a hindrance, he enables me. God's power is very personal. I may not know what to think or ask but he can do it because he is able. His grace is sufficient to meet the need (2 Corinthians 9:8). I can develop firmness and have a soft heart. Because God will keep me from stumbling and make me stand in his presence blameless with great joy (Jude 24). In him I put my trust for eternity.

I praise God for his hope (Psalm 16:9). In my super-sensitivity, I have discovered that I am secure in the Lord. No matter what happens, he is near. If God is for me, who can be against me? (Romans 8:31-32). God loves me and he is aware of every detail. No tribulation or distress or persecution will separate me from him (Romans 8:35). I can have complete rest in him. He will keep my heart safe. I will not be shaken.

Personal Response

CHAPTER 2

Jesus' Plan

I am a doer of the word (James 1:22). In my disastrous experience, my wife was killed and I was messed up. Do I have enough faith to deal with this experience? Is my faith genuine? I must keep my eyes upon the Savior who is "the author and finisher of our faith" (Hebrews 12:2). God's plan is that I have a firm conviction of truth. I have a personal surrender to God. I have conduct inspired by that surrender. "Faith is the substance of things hoped for, the evidence of things not seen" (Hebrews 11:1). The words 'substance' and 'evidence' emphasize foundation. The words 'hoped for' and 'things not seen' designate that which God has promised. Faith is that possession of the believer which gives him knowledge, assurance, and certainty. Faith is a response of trust in a person, based upon that individual's character and word, which issues in action.

My Responsibility

I will move forward as I practice faith. God's plan will work as I become responsible. My responsibility is to respond to God on the basis of what is said in the Scripture. I cannot earn the grace of God. I must "hear faith" (Galatians 3:2-3). My belief is not based on rules and forms, but believing and receiving the baptism of the Spirit by the "hearing of faith."

My Action

Faith is much more than an intellectual assent to a group of ideas. It is an action. The Bible says, "Remembering without ceasing your work of faith, and labor of love, and patience of hope in our Lord Jesus Christ, in the sight of God and our Father" (1 Thessalonians 1:3). Genuine faith is practice. It deals with the way I live. Every day, I must make a decision to accept God's will and glorify him. I will overcome as I love, be patient, and hope in Jesus Christ.

My Strength

My strength is nourished on the words of faith. These words refer to the basis of my faith in the scriptures. The word of God is the very foundation for what we are to believe as well as the blueprint. In my troubled time facing ill health from head to toe, the scripture has become my resource. Strength is provided (1 Timothy 4:6). I will and have attained. I am thankful for the Bible. It has truly been my source of strength.

My Warfare

I have been reminded that I have a fight on my hands. Since I belong to the Lord Jesus Christ, a war is going on. The devil hates the Savior and can only strike out at Him in His people. I also have a conflict with the world as well as my fleshly desires. I have to choose to praise the word of God. I will receive divine protection (1 Timothy 6:12). The Bible is powerful. It's a big exercise to see it in action. Through faith I am using His promise to obtain victory.

My Certainty

Doubt and fear will come into my presence. I have to learn that there is a union of the Scriptures and faith. There comes to pass a spiritual act whereby the promises of God and my faith are united and become one. Faith is the body of truth believed (2 Timothy 4:7). Faith is the response of submission, obedience and trust (John 1:12). There is a response of faith and the word of God united. My certainty is assured. I cannot separate the true act of believing from that which is believed.

My Relationship

Let's keep in memory that Jesus is the author and finisher of our faith (Hebrews 12:2). He has given me the gift of faith. He will sustain me. He makes it possible to enter into His presence in heaven. I live with trials, confusion, frustration and disappointment. But with a serious attempt, I can choose genuine faith.

My Possession

I am a doer of His word (James 1:22). I possess God's precious faith (2 Peter 1:1). The word precious shows me the value of faith. The highest value in life is spiritual. The most priceless benefits are found in grace. I want to be characterized with faith, love, and hope. Obedience fruitfulness, as well as joy and peace are included. Faith is Jesus' plan for me to succeed. Each thought will draw me closer to him.

Personal Response

CHAPTER 3

Jesus' Promise

I know the blessing of his presence. I have experienced his power. I will follow him every passing day. My journey has been successful because the Bible has brought success. As I travel back and forth in reading and re-reading "Discovering God's Favor", it has demonstrated that Holy Scripture is the book to follow and that it will achieve what it wants to achieve. I love the promise in Proverbs 21:21, "He that followeth after righteousness and mercy findeth life, righteousness and honor." It is not a matter of trying to be successful. Failure doesn't create discouragement either. The Bible says very clearly that it provides confidence because it produces its own success. I cannot stand and give honor to myself. I can only bow before a Holy God in worship and humility. He prepares the way and pushes me in it. We will face wars with the enemy and it is hard because he is invisible. He is a trained specialist in deceit. In all the transitions of my life, the Word" has given victory. I have written on God's sovereignty, his creation and salvation, and through his word, my own heart changed. It wasn't an intellectual accent to the gospel. I have written about my own alternative syndrome, death, communion with God and how his Word has brought relational steadfastness.

I even wrote about pre-adolescence and my teen years. Words like trust, commitment, submission, respect, resolve and sincerity play an important part in those years. It all was real because of his Word. I have been and will continue to thank God for his spiritual insight and sovereign-bestowed-spiritual awakening. I realize that many things I have tried to teach have been taught already. Maybe remembrance is what is important. I have, through the years, been taught many principles. For them to work in my life, I need to practice and remember them.

I have spent time writing about why I believe in the Bible. I have written about my pastoral/ministry, educational/music and para-church ministries. Through discipleship in God's Word, each ministry has been grounded. His Word has been the foundation to my ministry in music education. I belong to a teaching staff, do some tutoring and consultation. It has all been possible through God's providential Word. Building relationships and sharing the Word have been a blessing.

The subject of love and marriage, parental guidance and pastoral ministry insights have increased my confidence in God's Word because it works. The Word has brought me to interaction with God. Communication with our Father has brought immeasurable blessing. The promises of God have been a safety net encircling my life. It is exciting to read what the Bible says about itself. It is more exciting to put it into action.

Notice what it says in Psalm 19:7, "The law of the Lord is perfect, converting the soul." When I see the word 'law,' I think of Moses. His statue can be seen in Washington DC as "the great law giver." The law statement takes in the entire doctrine of God. The whole body of scriptural truth is found in the Bible. It is perfect because it is the testimony of God. It converts the soul. It brings restoration. This begins with faith in Jesus Christ which was accomplished in my life as a child. I simply took God at his Word and believed in Christ's death and resurrection for my deliverance. This has developed into a lifelong process of transformation (Romans 12:2). This caused a change in my inward nature. My mind (the center of logical reasoning, ethical judgment and moral awareness) was changed. It has become Christ-centered, not through my will, but God's transforming power. The Word has changed my life from the inside out. It all started in my childhood . . . praise God!

"The testimony of the Lord is sure, making wise the simple" (Psalm 19:7b). This is a declaration of truth and a statement of fact. It is a witness of God's story and is the precepts that God wants us to know. It is sure, safe, stable, secure, will not fail us, effective, trustworthy and absolute. Therefore, we can be wise. As I grew Into my teens, I already had established a relationship with Jesus Christ. When I entered that period of seeking questions and answers, I developed in my education. The Bible was a resource and absolute truth in my life. I began to rely upon what I learned. My code of ethics was found in his Word because it works.

"The statutes of the Lord are right, rejoicing the heart," (Psalm 19:8a). The Bible is God's story and is a document of importance. It is his rule for us. The precepts of God's Word are founded in his righteousness. His Word is not polluted or diluted. I have confidence in his Word for they are right. In my adulthood, I have had many opportunities to share the Word. In this book, I have shared some of the blessings. It has been a difficult time. The enemy has been there throwing darts at me. I started keeping a record of God's intervention. The column of rejoicing surpasses the attacks. His Word has been used against the enemy and has also been the answer to the seeking heart. I am appreciative to the Lord in providing the scripture. Claim it for your life, sit back and watch it work.

"The commandment of the Lord is pure, enlightening the eyes," (Psalm 19:8a). My life has been recreated and transformed through his Word. As simple as I am, the Word has provided a sure testimony. It has demolished the enemy through the power of God's Word (2 Corinthians 10:5). It is a sacred book and has brought much joy and peace. My eyes have been enlightened through his Word. In my older years, I have set my mind on things above. I think the writing of my book has challenged me to think about praiseworthy things. The promise I started this chapter with "He that followeth after righteousness and mercy findeth life, righteousness and honor" (Proverbs 21:21), has worked for me and will for you. Is he calling you? Listen! Can you hear his voice? Please follow him.

Personal Response

CHAPTER 4

Jesus' Power

I am a doer of the word (James 1:22). My heart is sick. I am lonely. I am hurting. I am sad. I am suffering. I need power to overcome.

Believe The Promise

The Bible says, "I give unto you power" (Luke 10:19). In these times everything is being realized, including the complete fulfillment of the words of Jesus, "the truth shall make you free" (John 8:32). I don't have to walk by the power of the enemy. No matter how I feel or my will determines, I have power over all the power of the enemy. Satan was conquered by Jesus Christ on Calvary's Cross.

Claim The Power

In my mortal body, the resurrection power of the Lord Jesus Christ is gloriously proved (Romans 8:11). He dwells in me and will quicken my body.

The spirit of resurrection dwells, therefore, in my mortal body, so that in my physical weaknesses and often hard trials I may claim the resurrection power of Jesus Christ. The eternal man is above his body; whether he lives or dies, he is the Lord's. I can trust God's power to be in charge.

Follow The Straight Path

The soul is the organ with which we feel, understand, and register all earthly things. The danger is great when I let myself be led by my feelings and emotions and allow the enemy to get in. He obscures my vision of Jesus. I have to allow God to judge by the sword of the Spirit (Hebrews 4:12). To confuse spirit and emotional things is to mix eternal and temporal things and this affords the enemy an entrance into my life. I have to receive and obey the word and let it judge me so that what is spiritual is divided from that which is emotional, and I will become a spiritual person. My spirit will be led by the spirit of God on a straight path.

My heart will become established with grace (Hebrews 13:9). I can't have a crippled soul which will cause a crippled character. I don't have to be negative, but positive. I have to look at my suffering from God's point of view. I have to be crucified with Christ (Galatians 2:20). If I am inwardly zero, I have room for victory in Jesus. I have power in Jesus to overcome. I was born to win.

Rest In Truth

The human spirit is the seat of the Spirit of God. My spirit registers in contrast to the soul eternal things. Therefore it is the goal of the enemy to lead my spirit into darkness so that it falls into despair. I have to trust on the Lord even when I feel nothing. I don't have to live in darkness. I can be victorious in Jesus' power. "I know that my Redeemer liveth" (Job 19:25).

"My grace is sufficient for you, for my strength is made perfect in weakness" (2 Corinthians 12:9-10). Continue in God's grace through reading additional materials in my Pastoral Health Care series:

- Discovering God's Sufficiency, (book 1), p. 57.
- Discovering God's Love (book 2), pp. 57, 137.

- Discovering God's Counsel (book 3), p. 8.
- Discovering God's Kingdom (book 4), p.57.

Supernatural power is received through saturating my thoughts with Jesus. Miracles have given evidence of Jesus' power. Evidence of Jesus' resurrection gives testimony of His power. A personal relationship with Jesus produces indwelling power. Tranquility will follow Jesus' power.

Personal Response

CHAPTER 5

Jesus' Perspective

Sometimes life is cruel, sometimes it is full of suffering, physically and psychologically, sometimes our life expectations fail, sometimes there is little meaning to life, sometimes there is desperation and despair and sometimes there is just a falling out in the realities of life. Hope in the scripture always is a confident expectation. The word carries with it no uncertainties. I can be sure of the faithfulness of God in fulfilling his promises. With hope, I have conviction and assurance. I want to become contagious with encouragement and endurance that springs from hope.

- People with longstanding problems need hope.
- People with peculiarly difficult problems need hope.

- People that have been misled in regards to their problems need hope
- People who are harassed by fear need hope
- People who hopes have been dashed repeatedly need hope.
- People that have tried and failed need hope.
- People that have dramatic changes in life need hope.
- People that have fallen into depression need hope.
- People who have suffered life shattering experiences need hope

When I find myself searching for help, I find it in the hope that I have in Jesus. I have learned through Psalm 39:1-13 my innermost thoughts toward the wicked should be confident and not complaining. I should not embarrass God with my tongue (v. 1-2). My innermost thoughts toward God should be honest and not with a bitter attitude. I must share my anguish and pain (v. 3-4). When I am searching for hope, my innermost thoughts toward myself should not be deceived. I have to learn God's perspective on life (v. 5-6). My innermost thoughts toward deliverance should be scripture directed (v. 7-13). I have learned that in despair, I can experience confidence (v. 7). I have learned that in confession I can be released (v. 8). I have learned that correction is needed sometimes (v. 9-11). I have also been comforted (v. 12-13). These thoughts have started the path to hope.

I am discovering with excitement that in Jesus Christ name, I can live with hope and obtain the help I need. He is worth believing. There is no one whose understanding of life has come close to his. Jesus is in the life changing business. All kinds of people have come to him . . . satisfied people, messed up people, sick people, injured people, forgotten people, despised people, admired people, worthy people and religious people. I have come to him. Jesus has been changing lives for two thousand years. I am learning to leap out of my skin into faith. It is a realization of less of me and more of him. Not only do I have to let go of self and replace self with him, but I have to learn to wait. This is the in between period. When I hold onto his promise, "My hope is in Jesus . . . hear my prayer, O Lord, listen to my cry for help" (Psalm 39:7,12). I know victory will come because he keeps to his word. Some adjustments have to be made during the waiting time for victory. As I apply the attributes of God to the names given to Jesus, I will be given help and hope.

His name is wonderful (Isaiah 9:6). I believe in an awesome God. He can make my life wonderful because he is wonderful. My first adjustment in obtaining help is believing that he is awesome. Wonderful things have happened, are happening and will continue to happen. It all starts with experiencing forgiveness of sin and the invasion of a whole new life. "Christ liveth in me" (Galatians 2:20). Believing in Jesus is required (Acts 16:31). He wants intimate fellowship. "I count all things to be loss in view of the surpassing value of knowing Christ Jesus my Lord" (Philippians 3:7-8). In knowing God is the most important thing I can accomplish. My goal is to know him so well that I can say, "I have received a spirit of adoption as sons by which I cry, "Abba! Father!" The word Abba is equivalent of daddy. It is a term of respect and endearment.

By knowing God, I can better understand how I am to live. As I contemplate God's attributes through his names, I have been promised strength, encouragement and help. I know God loves me. God is love and the one who abides in love abides in God and God abides in him (1 John 4:16). I am surrounded with his infinite person, power and glory (John 14:20). "And I will pray the Father, and he shall give you another comforter, that he may abide with you forever . . . I am in my Father, and ye in me, and I in you" (v. 16, 20). He says, "I am in you." He is more than with me — he is in me. He indwells in me. He also supplies in himself all that any soul will ever need in time or eternity. The union I have 'in Christ' is beyond my comprehension. The oneness that I have with Jesus means many things (John 17:20-23). My emphasis here is fellowship. It is awesome to say that I have an everlasting companionship with him in the place we live he abides. I am looking for the eternal security which starts here and now as I draw near to him. "To be in Christ" refers to my position-union with Christ. In believing, I have that relationship and possession of the divine. I am safe in his hands because I am associated with the creator-redeemer God. "Christ in me" refers to the transformation power.

His name is counselor. I believe in an all-knowing God. He is my counselor. He knows everything. "Who has directed the Spirit of the Lord or as his counselor has informed him? With whom did he consult and gave him understanding? And who taught him in the path of justice and taught him knowledge, and informed him of the way of understanding? (Isaiah 40:13-14). God knows what he knows simply because he knows it. He did not learn it. The second adjustment is to accept his counsel. He is qualified to counsel me. He is eternal God whom "dwelleth all the fullness of the Godhead bodily" (Colossians 2:9). Jesus Christ was a part of the eternal counsel of creation. He was there when the Father said, "Let us make man." He understands me because he became man. He is able to enter into the experiences that perplex and burden me. He knows my heart and mind. He is able to help me understand myself. I have to let go of my self and let him take over. I must sit back and learn to watch him work. He knows me, my feelings, desires and my personality and disease. He has known everything from the beginning (Acts 15:18). Nothing can escape his all-encompassing knowledge. I have learned that God permits trials for reasons we may or may not understand, but he is able to bring good out of even the worst circumstances. I am able to have confidence because he knows all the possibilities. He is personal. The Bible says, "O Lord, thou hast searched me and known me" (Psalm 139:1-2). He knows my thought process (Ezekiel 11:5). God is concerned about the details that he knows everything going on behind the scenes (Job 23:10).

His name is mighty God. I believe in a powerful God. Jesus is God himself There is nothing God cannot do. His unlimited power will reflect his divine glory and accomplish his sovereign will. "Power belongs to God" (Psalm 62:11). He is able to "call into being that which does not exist" (Romans 4:17). "He spoke and it was done" (Psalm 33:6). Nothing is impossible with God (Luke 1:37). The scripture says, "Thou has formed my inward parts..I am fearfully and wonderfully made" (Psalm 139:13-14). God's power is very personal. "Thy will be done" (Matthew 5) is my prayer. He is able to deliver (Daniel 3:17). He is able to keep me standing in his presence (Jude 24). He says be strong in the Lord and in the strength of his might (Ephesians 6:10). The third adjustment for change is the fact that he is "mighty God." He is called "Immanuel," God with us. I have to understand his claims and accept his deity. With that response, I am strengthened with all might. He takes care of the demands of life. No matter what the problem he has power to meet it, handle it, solve it, and use it for my good and his glory.

His name is everlasting Father. I believe in a sovereign God. He is the originator of eternity. I live in a new dimension of life. God has absolute rule and control over all of his creation. God rules absolutely over the affairs of men. God can do whatever he wants to do simply because it is all his. "The earth is the Lord's and all it contains, the world, and those who dwell in it" (Psalm 24:1). Everything that occurs does so under the hand of a sovereign God. The fourth adjustment for change is in his name, the everlasting Father. God has created me for eternity and Jesus Christ came to earth to reveal eternity (I John 1:1-2). There is more to life than what my senses reveal. In trusting Jesus, I am able to meet every detail of life with confidence. I am safe in Jesus because of who he is. I exist for him. I can live in confidence because Jesus provides strength. There are no chance happenings. Whatever happens, it will bring good (Psalm 8:28). He has the whole picture. I can trust in Jesus and he is able to guard what I have entrusted to him (2 Timothy 1:12).

His name is Prince of Peace. I believe in an intimate God. The fifth adjustment for change is peace. When I accomplish the alignment process through his grace, I will experience peace. Jesus brings peace because he is peace. Do not try to change the circumstances but change in character. Peace does not come from the outside in but in reality comes from the inside out. I am learning that my testing, trials and temptations can become a win-win situation. I must learn to let go of self. I must learn to make the adjustments. I must learn to practice the victory in peace. He is free from limitations of space. He is everywhere present. He is in me (I John 4:4). I believe in an awesome God because he is wonderful in all his acts. He wants fellowship with me. I believe in an all-knowing God because he provides wise counsel. He has all knowledge. He knows my inner needs. I believe in a powerful God because there is nothing he cannot do. I believe in a sovereign God because he is the originator of eternity. He is in control. When I reflect upon these facts and allow them to penetrate my spirit, soul and body, I am able to face today.

As I repeat the names of Jesus with a sincere heart and allow the Holy Spirit to enable me, I will be encouraged. This is a starting point. Authentic transformation takes time. It is a process. It is not a formula to follow. It is not some basic principles to apply. It is not a mechanical determination. It is faith working in me through the Holy Spirit's guidance and power. "May the God of hope fill you with all joy and peace as you trust in him, so that you may overflow with hope by the power of the Holy Spirit" (Romans 15:13).

The promise of help is provided through Jesus. I am thankful for the Lord's presence. This chapter was written when I started a new journey in my life. I am facing a fearful, dreadful, uncertainty in my health. The biopsy has returned with a positive result. Cancer is the disease. I was told that my cancer is the second killer of man. That information was really encouraging. I am waiting for the details and what treatment options I have. I can list some of them but do not like the side effects. I still need to know the facts. The initial shock has started to wear off. My family is very supportive. I know their prayers and spiritual perspective will continue to be helpful.

My daughter shared a prayer and Psalm 91:11- "He who dwells in the shelter of the most High will rest in the shadow of hie Almighty." She has started a network of prayer support. My son immediately gave me a verse from Hosea 6:3 - "Let us acknowledge the Lord . . . as surely as the sun rises he will appear . . . he will come to us." He has set up a network of prayer warriors. I am so pleased that they have accepted this challenge in the way that they have. They know what works and they know what pleases God. Both Bible references, without them knowing it, reinforce the verse the Holy Spirit gave to me and my wife - James 4:8 - "Draw near to God and he will draw near to you." My dark thoughts have turned to the light because Jesus is wonderful. My folly has turned to wise thinking because Jesus is my counselor. Losing heart has changed to a conquering spirit because Jesus is my mighty God. I have been drawing closer to my everlasting Father who holds eternity in his hands. When I think of these names of Jesus, peace from the Prince of Peace has entered my spirit. "Jesus is the sweetest name I know and he's just the same as his lovely name, and that's the reason why I love him so, O Jesus is the sweetest name I know."

Personal Response

CHAPTER 6

Jesus' Prayer

The Bible says, "He made us and we are his" (Psalm 100:3). This is a favorite Psalm of many followers of Jesus. It is a great doxology that is found in Psalm 100. I have used the verse many times to introduce my concerts. "Make a joyful noise unto the Lord" (Psalm 100:1). I thought at least I'm biblical if the instrumentalists sound like noise rather than music. We could divide the Psalm into five sermons. "Shout with praises to the Lord" is found in verse one. "Serve the Lord with gladness" is in verse two. My primary text is in verse three. It says "know that he is Lord". "Enter into his gates" is found in the fourth verse. The chapter ends with "receive his mercy."

During times of hardship, suffering, trials and the unknown, we can find rest. During my preparation for open-heart surgery, the doctor said to think about something good and this scripture came to my memory. It has continued to bring his power, presence and peace to my soul. It will do the same for you.

Can anyone fix our troubles? The answer is yes. We don't suffer apart from the knowledge of God. Do not be intimidated by all the talk. God knows all the details. Keep in mind God's character rather than his creation. He has the big picture in view. This is not a formula, remedy, prescription or cure. It is the course I have followed to conquer. Every day I have to affirm, accept and adjust to God's plan of action.

As far as I am concerned, the Bible is absolute in truth. In my deepest worry and concern, I have discovered the spiritual solution strategy works for me. I have been trained to look to the Holy Scriptures for answers. They have proved themselves as a profitable resource. I have found peace and rest when I did not think I would be able to. Just think of it . . . "people who know their God will display strength and take action" (Daniel 11:32). Let us study the text and experience strength, support and steadfastness.

We have to affirm God's intervention. In times of difficulties, it is hard to read, study or do research to find an answer. We may only be able to pray. This is the best reaction. I had to affirm that 'He' in the text refers to God. Pray the Lord's Prayer (Matthew 6:9-13) and put your own communication with it.

'Our Father' refers to our creator God. He is personal, intimate, self-existent, self-sufficient and eternal. Things do not just happen. He can do whatever he wants because it is all his (Psalm 24:1). There is no chance happening, no luck and no mistakes. Both good and bad fall under his control. He has absolute rule over the affairs of men. He is sovereign. He works all things after the counsel of his own will (Ephesians 1:11). We have a relationship with him through faith in his son (Romans 10:9-10). Forsaking all I trust him (a child's definition). I know he has my best interests in mind.

'Who art in heaven' — God is spirit. He exists everywhere at the same time. He is in us. We live, move and exist in him. We can be assured in our total dependence upon him because he is present.

His kingdom provides spiritual guidance through mercy, truth, righteousness, peace and harmony. Our citizenship is on the earth and in heaven. Our attitude on earth should be directed from heaven. God's residence is everywhere. Let's obtain our instruction from him and 'seek his kingdom' (Matthew 6:33).

'Hallowed be thy name' is the central attribute of God. All others stem from it. Respect, reverence, awe, appreciation, honor, glory, adulation and worship are included in this word. It is the doxology of the prayer. "Great is the Lord and greatly to be praised" (Psalm 57:11). This part of the prayer provides the equipment to accomplish that which follows.

'Thy name, kingdom and will be done on earth as it is in heaven' refers to his rules for us to follow. We need to be conscious of his presence. He has the plan for our lives. We have to learn to pray in his name which means we place his name on each request. We have to learn to allow him to reign in our lives. We have to replace our will for his will.

'Give us, forgive us and lead us' includes three kinds of prayers. We can bring our daily needs to him. He can provide for our well-being. He can take care of our emotional, physical, spiritual and directional concerns (Psalm 23). He wants us to be intimate with him. Confession of sin and adoration given to him will start the path to close fellowship. The third kind of prayer is intercession. This is when we forget ourselves and bring others to the attention of God. God wants to hear our requests.

'For thine is the kingdom and power and the glory forever.' This is the benediction in the prayer. We serve under his kingdom. We live with his strength. All our needs are met through him. In our struggles, we have to affirm who 'He' is. It will give us victory. He who dwells in the secret place of the most high shall abide under the shadow of the Almighty. He is our refuge and our fortress, in him we can trust (Psalm 91:1,2). The first step for endurance and overcoming is affirmation. His intervention will be felt.

We have to accept God's indwelling. In times of discomfort, discouragement, discontent, distress, depression and dread, we can be assured that he is working on our behalf. The Scripture teaches that God the Father (Ephesians 4:6), God the Son (Colossians 1:27), and God the Spirit (1 Corinthians 6:19), are within us. Christians have possession of the divine nature. The individual persons of the godhead lives and works through us (Romans 8:9). Our negatives are part of his positive program. God knows where he wants to take us and how he wants to get us there, God is near when we feel him and when we do not feel him. He counsels with his promises that he is going to accomplish something if we think so or not.

We have to accept that the 'us' in the text refers to our redeemer God that has become our substitute. He says "Come unto me (Matthew 11:28-30). These are life changing words, but they cannot be heard by our sinful, rebellious and stubborn minds without a sovereignly bestowed spiritual awakening. The divine initiative is in verse 27 and a free offer to all in verses 28-30 (*Discovering God's Favor*, JFG, p. 13). These are the steps to follow to trust Jesus. "All ye that labor and are heavy laden" are words that describe our condition. We have to recognize our sinful condition. The first element in trusting Jesus is total dependency. "And I will give you rest" — liberation is given through Jesus. We can entrust our spirit, soul and body to him because of who he is and whet he has done. He is the pre-existing Son of God who became man in order to reveal the Father and bring eternal life through his death and resurrection (John 20:30-31).

"Take my yoke upon you and learn of me, for I am meek and lowly in heart." A complete turnaround is necessary. Through Jesus, we can turn from sin and replace it with faith. This is not an intellectual exercise but a whole heart change.

"For my yoke is easy and my burden is light." The yoke is a symbol of submission and it is joyful. Salvation occurs when God changes the heart and unbelievers turn from sin to Christ (Colossians 1:13). Faith is the process for Jesus to enter the heart and dwell there (Ephesians 3:17). Genuine conversion involves five essential elements. We cannot interpret spiritual reality with human reason. We have to accept God's invitation as a child with a sense of dependency. The authority comes through the revelation of God. Man-made religion is fruitless and vain. Only by God's revelation from his son are we able to receive divine truth.

We cannot earn our salvation. Finding truth comes through Jesus which involves a complete turnaround. Faith is the flip side of repentance. We turn from sin to the Savior. It is a turning of the whole heart to Christ. Submission is found in the word "yoke" and discipleship in the words "and learn of me." Together they imply obedience (*The Gospel According to Jesus*, John F. MacArthur, Jr., p.115). The second step for endurance and overcoming is acceptance. His indwelling will be felt.

We have to make some adjustments through God's illumination when we suffer, become helpless, fear the unknown and are hopeless, decide to face life realistically and with absolutes. We know life is not a bed of roses. The spiritual solution strategy does work. After we affirm God's presence and accept his supernatural power through his son, we can learn to demonstrate the fruit of the spirit. Renewing our thinking process will take place.

We can be successful with a continual filling of the Holy Spirit (Ephesians 5:18). Remember, we are new creations in Jesus Christ (1 Corinthians 5:17).

Love is the highest of virtues. It has to be our priority. We can make the right decisions because God is in us. Meeting his conditions is necessary (Matthew 6:33). Loving with intensity will deepen our fellowship. It will produce a selfless, serving, sympathetic and secure heart. We can follow the example of the gospel writers. Matthew was a tax collector for Rome. He was despised and belonged with the outcast in the community. He was good at keeping records. He knew his Old Testament. He preached love through a changed life. He answered Jesus' call to follow. The feast he gave at his home was the means to share Jesus with others. His life after meeting Jesus was selfless. He looked at life from God's perspective rather than his own. Mark was brought up in a home of prayer. He was tutored by Peter, Paul and Barnabas. He demonstrated love through service.

Luke was well-trained and believed to be a physician. He was a companion of Paul. He examined all the authentic records and consulted every available eyewitness. He speaks of the humanity of Jesus and shared his love through having a sympathetic heart.

John speaks of the divinity of Christ. He gives a theological rather than a biographical or historical presentation of the person of Christ. He was with Jesus constantly. What he experienced under the teaching of Jesus Christ proved that he was God incarnate. He demonstrated love through having a secure heart.

Love will produce joy in spite of suffering and adverse circumstances. Various trials will come but our sovereign God is in charge. He knows what we can bear (1 Corinthians 10-13). We have to choose to receive joy through obedience and faith. Joy is a divine happiness that undergirds all emotional reactions. It is a life of enthusiasm and beauty. A relationship with Jesus Christ, a growing fellowship with a sovereign God and worship with the Holy Spirit will lead the way. God is working in us. We have to yield our agenda for the day to Him. He is the boss. We have to make decisions in his will. Joy will be the end result. The adjustments are hard to accomplish because the flesh is weak. The peace of God will become reality. We have to accept the authority of Jesus (Hebrews 1:1,2). Believing the supernatural is not through the natural, it is developing through the supernatural. God has fully expressed himself in Christ (John 3:16). We cannot be careless in our effort to follow Jesus. We must have a deliberate desire. The third step for endurance and overcoming is making the adjustments. His illumination will be felt.

The Bible says, "He made us and we are his. (Psalm 100:3). God the Father has chosen us, God the Son has purchased us and God the Holy Spirit has sealed us. According as he hath chosen us," (Ephesians 1:4) this means to pick out for one's self. (Wuest's word study, p.30). The word "elect" in 1 Peter 1:2 is the noun form of the verb "chosen." God knows everything by virtue of who he is. God's knowledge and eternal purpose intersects with human choice in such a way that we have real choices to make and yet those choices fulfill God's purposes to accomplish his goal. God does make provisions for all but he has elected some, leaving us with a choice but guarantees his plans (*Awesome God*, Tony Evans, p. 145). "To whom we have redemption through his blood, the forgiveness of sins, according to the riches of his grace," (Hebrews 1:7-8). we have been released from sin. The word "sin" means to step aside. Grace is God's awesome favor. His grace provides the power to overcome our difficulties. He gives us wisdom and understanding. We have been sealed with the Holy Spirit of promise (Ephesians 1:13). The seal is the Holy Spirit. It is a finished transaction. We have his permanent residence. We are eternally secure. The pure grace of God brings about the fruitfulness. Our creator God has chosen us, our redeemer God has purchased us and our comforter God has sealed us. We are 'His Very Own' (our theme song).

Personal Response

CHAPTER 7

Jesus' Prescription

"One thing I ask of the Lord that I may dwell in the house of the Lord all the days of my life, to gaze upon the beauty of the Lord and to seek him in his temple. For in the day of trouble, he will keep me safe ... my heart says of you, seek his face! Your face, Lord, I will seek" (Psalm 27:4-5, 8). My soul is secure as long as I gaze upon the Lord. This means with intensity. In the previous verses a strong affirmation of confidence has been recorded. 'The Lord is my light and my salvation, whom shall I fear" (v. 1-3). The New Testament counterpart to this is "If God be for us, who can be against us" (Romans 8:31). My life is and will continue to be wrapped with his arms (v. 4-5). As I gaze upon the Lord, I will have a sense of his protection and will not worry but music will flow into my heart (v. 6).

With intensity, I will gaze upon the Lord. Some people think that Jesus was just God. Some people think that he was just man, and some people say that Jesus was an angel. Some think that he was an angel and man. I believe that Jesus was and is God incarnate which means that he is both God and man. Jesus was born of a human mother (Galatians 4:4). He grew up like any other human being (Luke 2:52). He hungered (Matthew 4:4) and was thirsty (John 19:28). He grew weary and needed rest (John 4:6). He felt sadness and cried (John 11:33-35). He suffered (John 19:1), died (John 19:33), and was buried (John 19:40-42). He was human in every sense that we are, yet he was without sin (Hebrews 4:15).

As I gaze upon the Lord, I have discovered that he is one person who has two natures, human and divine. Jesus, God the Son, existing as the second person of the triune God, united his divine nature to a human nature and through it came into the world. He did not stop being God when he added humanity to himself. Remember, God has no limitations. We are "one-dimensional beings" and he is not. In Deuteronomy 6:4, it says "Yahweh, our God, Yahweh is a plurality within an indivisible unity." God is one divine nature shared by three persons — the Father, Son and Holy Spirit. God the Son having an infinite nature assumed in addition a finite nature. There is one divine nature or essence of God. In Jesus Christ, we have added a human nature. Jesus is the Son of God (Lord) and Son of Man (Savior).

I have gazed upon Jesus through looking at his true identity, through studying the miracles in prophecy, through observing the miracles in his life, through his sinless life, through the testimony of close witnesses and through his resurrection. The evidence is there to be believed but as Jesus said, "If they do not listen to Moses and the prophets, they will not be convinced even if someone rises from the dead" (Luke 16:31).

As I gaze upon Jesus, I am convinced that Jesus Christ can do whatever he wills to do according to his character. Jesus is my spiritual and physical healer. Whatever my needs are, he already knows about them. He knows how I will react or act toward them. He knows what works for me. He knows what is best for me. My decision is simply, "Thy will be done." My responsibility is to gaze upon Jesus intently. In my intense search, he will make me free in whatever my need is. He said, "If you remain in my word, you are truly my disciples and you will know the truth and the truth will make you free." (John 8:31-32).

In my gazing upon Jesus, I have confidence in him because of who he is. If I learn to do what he says to do, I will have continual assurance of his presence, power and peace. These characteristics will be flowing through my veins because I have learned to take his perspective in all things. Real hope for me is freedom and growth found in God's grace. Everything I have been writing about seems to be a mystery. It works if I gaze upon Jesus and obey his word. The Scripture starts with "If you . . . " I must respond with my head and heart to the gospel. In my childhood, I received Jesus into my life and began a growing relationship. The Christian walk is hard and can be a struggle because the old nature is fighting against it. I have and will continue to relinquish my will to Jesus because true liberation comes when my heart says yes to God's words "follow me."

It works as I gaze upon Jesus and obey his word. The Bible says, "If you remain in my word." My greatest interest is to absorb the Bible into every activity of life. Dependency upon God will result in constructive actions, not destructive ones. Craving his word is a necessity. The Holy Spirit provides that craving through my yieldedness.

It works if I gaze upon Jesus and obey his word. His word says, "and you will know the truth." The old behavior can change with diligence and discipline. I have to apply his word to my life. Transformation is a process and I have to learn the tricks of the mind and old nature. God's intervention will take place.

It works if I gaze upon Jesus and obey his word. "And the truth will make you free." Everything I do involves some kind of dedication. Making a resolution will not work. Trying to reform will not work. Taking a pain pill will reduce the pain but will not provide a cure. The grace of God sets me free.

Dynamic DOER

My energies are enabled by God's empowerment. My willingness to participate through faith will bring victory. Faith is making a decision according to God's word.

Personal Response

CHAPTER 8

Jesus' Priority

The more I think upon God's Word, the more I will think like God. His view of things will become my views and his attitudes will become mine. Knowing God's will causes me to pray in his will. It is exciting to explore the vastness of an infinite God. It is also exciting to see how I am wonderfully made (Psalm 139:14). Through my situation, I am more conscious of how the brain and heart work. The situation and the knowledge of God must be transferred to the heart. The brain and heart oversee complex systems that are necessary for life, the nervous system and the circulatory system. Each is encased in a protective fortress of calcium, one inside the cranium and the other within the rib cage. They are on the job all the time with no days off until death or the resurrection day. The human brain is the single most complex apparatus of all God's vast creative genius. It is the center of my nervous system and contains billions of neurons, each having thousands of synoptic connections.

The heart is smaller than my brain but no less impressive. In an average lifetime, the heart contracts and relaxes two and a half billion times without stopping to rest. In every heart, blood is drawn into my heart, filtered, processed and pumped back out again to every millimeter of my body. The brain is the center of my thinking and the heart represents my affection, emotion, and personality. I have to learn to love the Lord with all my heart and to keep my heart with all diligence for out of it springs the issues of life (Proverbs 4:23). Sometimes it is hard to get the message from head to heart.

The knowledge of God has to filter down into the heart. It takes nourishment from God's Word through observation, interpretation and application. I have to inform my thinking through contemplation. I will then understand his perspectives. I am all set as I respond to the text,

Dynamic DOER

"What think ye of Christ" (Matthew 22:42). I am learning to be a doer of the Word (James 1:22). This is absolutely necessary for me. My heart stopped pumping blood as a matter of fact during surgery. A life machine kept it pumping. After four bypasses and some valve work, it started to work on its own again. The nervous system, circulatory system, rib cage and the emotions and personality have all been affected. I discovered that the supernatural power of God can be infused through me through the Holy Spirit. The saturating of God's Word through accepting its authority, applying it and and studying it will make me think like God.

The Bible says, "And he reasoned in the synagogue and persuaded the Jews and Greeks, and he continued teaching the Word of God among them" (Acts 18:4,11). I know of no other way to give the authority of the Scriptures than to continue teaching the word. I would like to reason and persuade you that the Scriptures are a living, vital agency with supernatural power in itself. Read the promise, "For as the rain cometh down and the snow from heaven, and returneth not thither, but watereth the earth and maketh it bring forth and bud, that it may give seed to the sower and bread to the eater; so shall my word be that goeth forth out of my mouth. It shall not return unto me void, but it shall accomplish that which I please, and it shall prosper in the thing whereto I send it" (Isaiah 55:10-11). To the same purpose Jeremiah has written, "Is not my word like a fire? saith the Lord; and like a hammer that breaketh the rock in pieces?" (Jeremiah 23:29). God uses his word, "For the word of God is quick and powerful and sharper than any two-edged sword, piercing even to the dividing asunder of soul and spirit and of the joints and marrow, and is a discerner of the thoughts and intents of the heart" (Hebrews 4:12).

The Bible is an ancient book for modern times. It is one book, one history and one story and one mind produced it. God himself became a man so that we might know what to think when we think of God. I could give all the evidences for scriptural authority but why don't you read the Bible for yourself and let it prove itself? The Bible says, "As newborn babes, desire the sincere milk of the word, that ye may grow thereby" (1 Peter 2:2). God has given his word so that believers may grow thereby. We have not fulfilled our obligations to the word until application has taken place. The Bible is not only the source book for information but has life-changing power for today. Growth in the spiritual life comes not merely from hearing but from hearing and doing. The Bible says, "the effectual doer shall be blessed in what he does" (James 1:25). "If you know these things, you are blessed if ye do them" (John 12:17).

The Bible has been given so that man's basic nature can be changed. "All scripture is given by God and is profitable for teaching, for reproof, for correction, for training in righteousness, that the man of God may be adequate, equipped for every good work" (2 Timothy 3:16-17). It teaches, rebukes, restores and trains for righteous living. It equips us to do the work that God wants us to do. The Bible convicts, regenerates, nurtures, cleanses, counsels, guides, prevents sin, revives, strengthens, gives wisdom, delivers and helps. The Bible alone realistically and sufficiently meets man's deepest problems, longings, needs and inadequacies. It provides the answers to man's needs for deliverance from the penalty of sin, for spiritual progress for victory, for guidance and for the personal relationships and conduct. As we learn the Scriptures, let us apply it to our daily activities.

The Bible says, "Blessed are the undefiled in the way, who walk in the law of the Lord" (Psalm 119:1). What is wrong with reading the Bible? Why do people think it so strange? Some people have the idea that the Bible is just for the mentally weak, for the ignorant and some imagine that it is just for the shut-ins or only for the children. Why do the teens and young adults turn from it? I believe they do not go on to read it, believe it, study it or follow it. If we are going to walk in the law of the Lord, we must follow this pattern.

We need to study it through and master a verse every day. Think of it and the end of the year, you will have 365 verses in your heart and mind to bring about happiness, direction, peace and contentment. We need to pray about it. We must let each verse become a part of our very being, praying the verse into reality and then seeing the promises of God, as we claim them, change our lives. We must write down our thoughts. We cannot remember everything but our computer mind has it and we need to refresh our memory. That, of course, brings us to working it out. Let the Bible get in your heart and then live it out every day. It is not good only to study it through or pray about it or put it down or work it out, but we must also pass it on. We must talk about it. Let the Word of God inspire and bless your heart. This takes discipline. You cannot be lazy. Walk in the law of the Lord and you will be saturated with his thoughts.

Personal Response

CHAPTER 9

Jesus' Path

I am a doer of the Word (James 1:22) How do we obtain control of our body, mind and will, so that God will be glorified?

Enemy without: We have responsibility to control our bodies. We must guard what stimulates our desires. We should crave the Word of God (1 Peter 2:2), not what sinful men do (1 John 2:16). We need to develop a thinking process that doesn't gratify our physical desires (Romans 13:14).

Enemy within: We have responsibility to control our thought lives. We must guard what influences our minds. We need to keep in mind that we are what we think we are (Proverbs 23:7). We must think the standards and evaluate what we think by activating God's word in our lives (Philippians 4:8).

Ultimate choice: We have responsibility to identify with Christ and demonstrate His character, not sinful patterns (Ephesians 4:20-24). We must delight in His will (Psalm 40:8) and submit our will to God (James 4:7).

We need to develop a renewed mind (Romans 12:2) and set our affections / desires on things above (Colossians 3:1). With this direction, wisdom, understanding and discretion will guard us from evil (Proverbs 2:10-12).

Our bodies, minds and wills can be in control daily as we practice faith, obedience and perseverance with conviction and confidence.

The *key* to having control in body, mind and will is unconditional surrender. We have to learn whenever sin is discovered, it instantly must be confessed and renounced/ Too often, we indulge, tolerate and excuse sin. Deliverance comes through absolute honesty with God about our spiritual condition.

The *act* of surrender involves *yieldedness*. We have to be conscious of God's nearness and maintain a spirit of yielding our body, mind and will to Him daily . . . our flesh, intellect, and emotion belong to Him. This process will start as we acknowledge our sin (Romans 12:1-2).

The *necessity* of surrender involves *repentance*. We have to be conscious of our inadequacy. A decision to turn around and allow God to really change us must take place. Disappointment - not success - will be the result if we continue to rest in our own abilities. We have to acknowledge His ownership (John 15:4).

The *attitude* of surrender involves *dependence*. Continuous victory will be the result of yieldedness, repentance, and dependency. It starts with simple trust and a believing dependence and assurance of a relationship with God through His son Jesus Christ (Romans 10:9-10). This is followed by learning to commit every matter to Him. We learn through the study of scripture and experiential faith . . . believing that in Christ nothing is impossible. Whatever our circumstances, He is able (2 Timothy 1:12).

The *satisfaction* of surrender involves *trust*. Living a life of surrender is not dependent upon a strong self-discipline but a life of faith. It is a life of rest and intense activity of the soul. To accomplish this, we must rely on and personally involve ourselves with this well-known text: "The Lord is my shepherd, I shall not want" (Psalm 23:1). As we analyze the verse and apply all that has already been said, it will provide the assurance that if we do what the Scripture says, we will have taken the offensive and will have control.

"*The Lord*" is my sovereign God. I am assured that I am in his providential care. He is in control. My responsibility is simply to surrender to Him.

"*Is my*" brings action to the text. Personally, I must make a decision to respond to His word (This is faith). The whole counsel of His Word is necessary.

"*Shepherd*" brings comfort. As lost and foolish people, we do have a leader that will guide us and take care of us even if we mess up.

"*I shall*" requires a personal decision with a definite response. It is a legal emphasis — a solid declaration.

"*Not want*" brings satisfaction and control of our body, soul and spirit if we respond to God and surrender to His will.

Personal Response

CHAPTER 10

Jesus' Prophecy

The Bible says, "If any man's work abide, he will receive a reward" (1 Corinthians 3:14). I know that if my work is deeply committed to Jesus Christ, it will be successful. I have received rewards and have been honored. I am working on the following rewards. Join me and bring glory to our Savior and Lord. I am working on this because I love Him. Man-made rewards are nice but can't be measured against God's.

"Every man that striveth for the mastery of the old nature has self-control" (1 Corinthians 9:25). "Truth shall spring out of the earth and righteousness shall look down from heaven" (Psalm 85:11). **Self-discipline** is the practice of obedience which will produce righteous conduct. The seeking heart is a must. Spiritual intimacy is a must. Relying on God is a must. Confession is a must.

"Your presence in the Lord's coming is my hope and joy" (1 Thessalonians 2:19). "All that the Father giveth me shall come to me" (Romans 8:29-30). "I am not ashamed of the gospel of Christ, for it is the power of God unto salvation" (Romans 1:16). "I must work the work of him that sent me, while it is day; the night cometh when no man can work" (John 9:4). The work starts with these words: "Come to me" (Matthew 11:28-30). I responded to them at seven years of age. I started to witness with American Sunday School Union with my family. As a teenager, I continued with my own Teen Age Gospel Team. In my young adulthood I traveled in the State of Michigan. **Self-determination** is involved and it works.

I am thankful for these words "I will send the Holy Spirit to you" (John 16:7-15). "Blessed is the man that endureth temptation" (James 1:12; 1 Corinthians 10:13). "We are the temple of the Holy Spirit (1 Corinthians 6:19). The leader of my life is the indwelling Holy Spirit. I am able to succeed. I have to learn to do what he wants. I have to be sensitive to his presence. I have to stop resisting God's Spirit. I have to stop saying no to his guidance. I have to stop refusing to yield to the work of God. I have to be in a constant attitude of yieldedness rather than rebellion. When I do these things, I am following him (Colossians 3:16). My desire is to be dominated by the Holy Spirit, not myself. **Self-dedication** will sustain trials and bring victory. God is ready to restore even when I have missed the mark.

Jesus Christ became a constant companion. Every day, I learn that I can live with His strength. I can rest in Him. I will not be shaken. These words have taken me through: 1 Peter 5:4. "You will receive a crown that fadeth not away." This refers to good shepherds of God's flock. It is a life that is not wasted and foolish. "The Holy Spirit shall be on you" (John 14:17). All my decisions stem from my eternal kingdom mindset. I preached my first sermon in my childhood to the community kids. I preached my last sermon to a church attendance 10,000 to a membership class.. Sometimes **Self-discomfort** is in the picture but it will produce a good shepherd. I am steadfast in the Lord's appearing (2 Timothy

4:8). I love him because he first loved me (1 John 4:19). He made me and I belong to him (Psalm 100:3). God's love is found in eternity past and eternity future. It has no end. Nothing can separate me from His love. I am driven by a person within. Genuine love is produced through the indwelling of the Holy Spirit. God has provided love (Genesis 1:27; 2:24). He has provided faith (1 Thessalonians 1:3). Self-Discovery will produce the real me. I choose to follow Jesus Christ (Faith). I give him his rightful place in my life (Love), and apply this to my future (Hope).

Jesus' prophecy is in the future but it starts now. The rewards are:

- Faithful Servant: 1 Corinthians 3:14
- Seeking righteousness: 1 Corinthians 9:25.
- Sharing faith: 1 Thessalonians 2:19.
- Sustain trials: 1 Corinthians 10:13.
- Studious Shepherd: 1 Peter 5:4.
- Steadfast appearance: 2 Timothy 4:8.

This completes my 'dynamic doer' challenge.

Personal Response

Acknowledgements

I appreciate all the people that God has used to influence me. Many of these thoughts have come to my memory over the past seventy-nine years through sermon notes, lectures, conversations, meditations and reading. I have not knowingly withheld any significant reference from others in my devotional. To the best of my knowledge, all statements and information are true and correct and given credit. Everyone I have come in contact with should be given credit. Pastoral Health Care and Divine Dialogue Series is a constant source of encouragement.

About the Author

John F. Gillette's story begins and ends with a song he sang in his childhood, "His Very Own, Wonderful Grace in His Word is made known, chosen by the Father, purchased by the Son, sealed by the Spirit, I am his very own." His desire every day is to glorify the Lord Jesus Christ in health and in sickness. He has learned every moment needs to be in God's presence.

Divine dialogue is a developmental process. He has been a lifelong student of the Scriptures. It is easy to fail the standards of God but he has an inner passion that he calls "the holy urge" to encourage him to go forward. His studies have been in the liberal arts but always guided through

About the Author

his biblical deep rooted foundation. His graduate research has been in religion and leadership.

He has served Jesus Christ since his childhood with diversity, independence and confidence in education, pastorate and leadership. His pastoral health care discovery series was published to help himself and minister to others that are having struggles in making spiritual, psychological and physiological adjustments.

More Books in the Series:

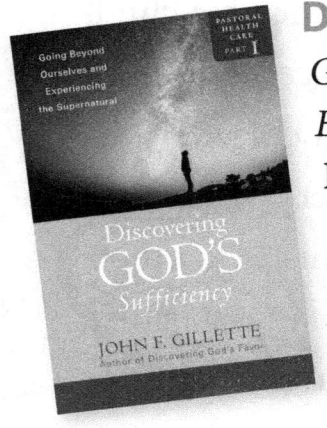

Discovering God's Sufficiency
Going Beyond Ourselves and Experiencing the Supernatural
Pastoral Health Care—Part One

Can anyone fix our troubles? The answer is 'yes.' How do we conquer our trials? We have to affirm God's intervention. We have to accept God's indwelling. We have to make some adjustments through God's illumination. We can experience God's power, presence and peace.

Discovering God's Love
Confirming God's love through the evidence of historical facts
Pastoral Health Care—Part Two

We can obtain strength to conquer through a knowledge of the 'Gospels' and receiving Jesus Christ into our hearts. The New Testament books of history give evidence of God's love. Through his love and faith, we are able to be strengthened, experience his support and become steadfast.

Available at www.schulerbooks.com/chapbook-press

Discovering God's Counsel
Applying his spiritual solution to meet difficult trials
Pastoral Health Care—Part Three

Dark days can be life threatening. We have to develop an adequate level of spiritual, psychological and physiological adjustments. We can live with confidence in God's sufficiency.

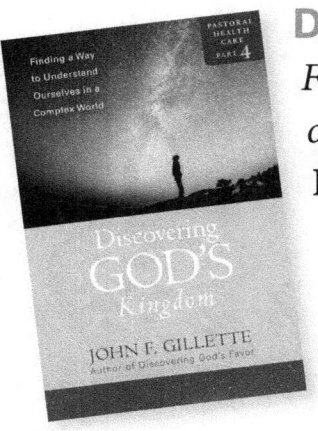

Discovering God's Kingdom
Finding a way to understand ourselves in a complex world
Pastoral Health Care—Part Four

Dealing with life, death, heaven and eternity with God's perspective is necessary. It involves a personal decision of belief, trust and faith. Knowledge and commitment will bring comfort and security. The eternal destiny directive will provide the way.

Available at www.schulerbooks.com/chapbook-press

Discovering God's Heart

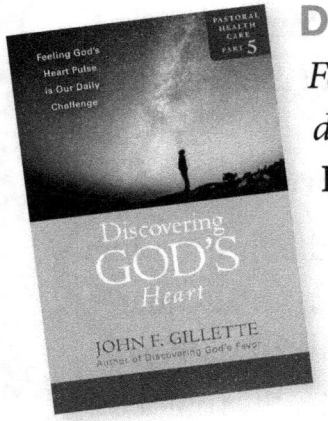

Feeling God's heart pulse is our daily challenge

Pastoral Health Care—Part Five

We have to practice the principles in the pastoral health care meditation method. We can handle any situation through thinking biblically. The spirit, soul and body are involved. Therefore, a holistic approach has to take place.

Available at www.schulerbooks.com/chapbook-press

www.ingramcontent.com/pod-product-compliance
Lightning Source LLC
Chambersburg PA
CBHW070241090526
44586CB00035B/1375